Invaluable Tips for Navigating & Succeeding with Family Court Processes as a Non-Attorney

Sean Gentile's Handbook for Family Court Processes

Sean Gentile

AuthorHouse™
1663 Liberty Drive
Bloomington, IN 47403
www.authorhouse.com
Phone: 833-262-8899

Because of the dynamic nature of the Internet, any web addresses or links contained in this book may have changed since publication and may no longer be valid. The views expressed in this work are solely those of the author and do not necessarily reflect the views of the publisher, and the publisher hereby disclaims any responsibility for them.

Any people depicted in stock imagery provided by Getty Images are models, and such images are being used for illustrative purposes only.
Certain stock imagery © Getty Images.

This book is printed on acid-free paper.

ISBN: 979-8-8230-0865-5 (sc)
ISBN: 979-8-8230-0864-8 (e)

Library of Congress Control Number: 2023909561

Print information available on the last page.

Published by AuthorHouse 05/17/2023

authorHOUSE®

FOREWORD

"This book is dedicated to those we gratefully serve."

Sean Gentile, MBA
2023

Sean Gentile has dedicated her life to helping people through family court processes. She is an author, businesswoman, and Family court mediator who inspires parents to persevere through the resistance of a spouse, a bureaucracy, and a court system. The main goal is to create a healthy emotional environment for the children involved and co-parent with success as one navigates through a challenging system.

Sean Gentile's Non-Attorney Divorce office is located in Oakland Park, Florida, and her team has assisted thousands over 23 years. It is open seven days a week from 8 am to 8 pm. Sean specializes in caring for each person who seeks help.

"I like people to see the joy in uncovering powerful information so they can command the show every step of the way with results." Sean Gentile

And to accomplish this, Sean's dedicated work ethic and energy sees each customer through with knowledge, respect, and inspiration.

TABLE OF CONTENTS

INTRODUCTION

Using this book should help you learn how to persevere in the family court and the child support bureaucracy. It can help you by learning that resistance is normal for workers in this system, and you must have the tenacity to move through it to accomplish your goals.

Learning tips for managing your emotions, getting everything in writing, and following up with time frames can help you with added support to accomplish a healthy result. Some healthy results are a win/win co-parenting agreement, mutual respect, validating your child's feelings, and being kind to yourself.

Understanding what you are up against may help to quell the frustration.

So use your strength to commit to achieving success through these practical tips.

Sean Gentile, MBA

Florida Supreme Court Family Mediator

ASK FOR THE GALAXY

WHEN BOTH PARENTS ARE GETTING ALONG, it is normal to agree to split the cost of the child's expenses. Most amicable parents understand a 50/50 split if both are earning a similar income.

Some child's expenses you would split are summer camp, aftercare, school trips, cell phone usage, health insurance, and school supplies including uniforms.

In the same way you would split the financial costs, you would also even out the time share with the child to 50/50 overnights as well. There are many variations to a 50/50 time share which both parents can review based on scheduling needs.

However, WHEN PARENTS DISAGREE, it is very common during divorce and/or child support matters that not only do parents strongly disagree they downright declare war.

When this happens, it is important to understand to work with issues that can be taken off the table in a negotiation. For example, you ask for 100% of the time with the child in addition to the Earned Income Child Tax Credit. The other parent disagrees with you having 100% time share. You then may negotiate down to 60/40 or 50/50, and parents alternate every other year with the Earned Income Child Tax Credit.

It is more advantageous to start from the top by asking for the entire galaxy, then you can negotiate down. If you start at 50/50 time share, you may end up with every other weekend, which is a minuscule amount of time with your child. Govern yourself accordingly and be assertive with your requests.

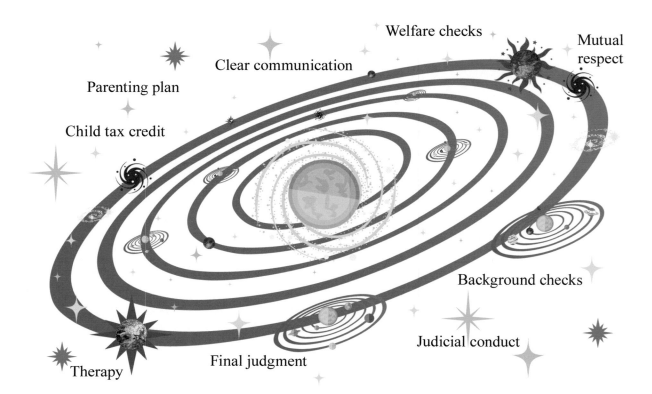

Welfare checks

Mutual respect

Clear communication

Parenting plan

Child tax credit

Background checks

Judicial conduct

Therapy

Final judgment

ACT LIKE AN ACTIVIST AND BE YOUR OWN ADVOCATE

How I define being an activist for my clients is to be able to respond effectively in areas that matter within your court case and to foster your child's best interest.
For example:

1. You must take care of yourself first.

When you are overwhelmed with feelings, seek assistance from a therapist and set small goals to forge a path to move on after your breakup.

2. Delegate and hire out for your housecleaning, car cleaning, or projects to lighten your load and make your life more manageable.

3. Join a support group. Young people going through divorce or family court matters could get additional support by joining a group, whether a grief group or a parenting group, to get that added support and make more connections. In addition, you may find someone you respect; hence, form a healthy friendship.

4. Background checks. Always understand as much as you can about the other parent's living environment. For example, if they get a new significant other, you may do background checks on that person, and keep documented information for when you need it. Your child's best interest should be at the top of your list. The child should always be in a safe environment free from drugs and alcohol.

5. Be perseverant in all that you do. For example, read up on good nutrition for your child. Extra educational resources or tutoring ensures your child gets maximum benefit from her education.

Overall, address all areas of your child's life fiercely to protect and allow your child to flourish.

The ability to act keeps everything governed correctly. You can do it.

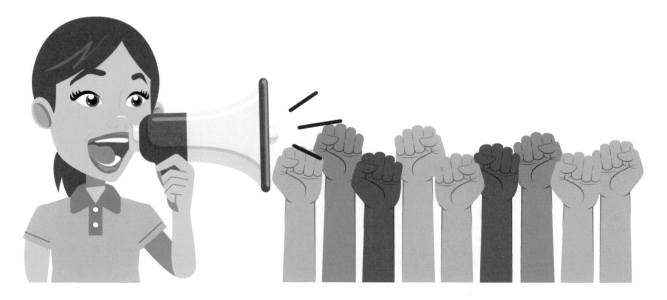

BUREAUCRATIC EFFECTIVENESS

Here are some ways that may be helpful when interacting with the child support office, courts, or other agencies.

1. Get the name and email of the top manager of the agency you're working with. Usually, there is a local manager and one who governs statewide.

2. Next, for whomever you're working with, obtain their name and email and copy all correspondence to the top managers as well.

3. In your email, here are some communication tips for effectiveness:

"Please highlight your answers from our meeting."

"When can I expect a report on your findings?"

"When can I expect a follow-up with the manager?"

"Here are the concerns regarding the child for the welfare check."

"Please indicate what law or procedure you are referring to."

"I expect to see your procedure manual to validate your information."

"Did they interview everyone concerning the child?" *(When doing a welfare check)*

"I need to see backup info."

4. For Court: Understand the arena you are in. The judge and or magistrate has codes of conduct to follow. Read up on the judicial code of conduct, and if you get the impression you cannot utter a word in the courtroom, respectfully ask, "According to the code of judicial conduct, when may I speak about the facts of the case?" No matter who is talking to you, check it out with backup data.

5. In-person meetings: Meet with the manager of the agency. Ask for all info in writing. Ask for backup procedures of that agency. Schedule follow-ups to ensure it is done.

6. Solve glitches: If things that are promised don't get done, call your local press writer who focuses on that agency. Give the writer the manager's name and the issue you are having. If you need more backup, organize a rally and let the department manager who failed to produce what you asked know you are doing the rally and that you will move forward with national coverage if needed until the manager's promise is fulfilled.

Lastly, if the press won't write about the agency's failings, write your own story and distribute it to apply more pressure.

7. Comprehend the psychology of a bureaucratic worker. Again, it helps to know what you're dealing with.

8. Hook up with an activist. Activists have a personality that doesn't require external approval. They are tough as nails and flourish with pressure and confrontation. They are the ones you want to know to fight the impenetrable walls of some bureaucracies.

9. Stay the course because you owe it to yourself.

WELFARE CHECKS

It is the responsibility of the child's parents and, frankly, our society in general to assure the safety of all children.

When your child is away at the other parent's home, and you are concerned, you may utilize the abuse hotline and law enforcement services via a welfare check.

The abuse hotline has certain guidelines regarding abuse. However, certain aspects of negative parenting can eventually lead to what the abuse hotline considers abuse. Therefore, keep a close eye on the other parent's parenting skills or lack thereof.

EXTREME ABUSE

* Violence in the home

* Sexual abuse

* Drug abuse

* Alcohol abuse

* Insidious vulgar name-calling

ABUSE

* Transient living

* Not allowing the child to be on time for school

* Not allowing the child proper sleep

* High sugar diet/Improper nutrition

* Withholding food

* Showing favoritism to other siblings

* Lack of grooming for the child

* Not providing age-appropriate clothing

* Not encouraging a variety of interests

* Not providing help if the child is doing poorly at school

* Improper car, no seatbelts, no car seats, etc.

A WELFARE CHECK

The situation that you are concerned about may or may not qualify for the welfare check. There are guidelines that the bureaucracy follows. You may request to speak to a supervisor to detail what you are concerned about clearly. Whether or not the agency supervisor decides to give the go-ahead, you still may have options. For example, you could call the police instead.

Be consistent and follow up.

THE BEST TIME to call for a welfare check is to examine the parent's schedule and have the welfare check when there are people in the house. For example: If the other parent has a regular workday schedule and will be home at the dinner hour, then it may be in your best interest and the child's best interest to conduct the welfare check at that time.

*The opinions expressed here are those of Sean Gentile, MBA, Florida Supreme Court Family Mediator, non-attorney, and her lengthy experience with Family issues. It does not substitute any legal advice or changes in any bureaucratic procedures.

MANAGE YOUR EMOTIONS

Feelings are there for a purpose. We respect the fact that we are human when we allow ourselves to feel and validate our feelings. And that is necessary for healthy human development. However, it is essential to understand that many who choose to ignore feelings end up postponing necessary actions and may excuse ample abuse by others.

One way to manage emotions is to acknowledge what is going on. For example: If you feel sad or betrayed over a divorce, recognize your humanness and get some support. There are "grief groups" or counseling for that precious support during this trying time. In a grief group, a facilitator may reference important reading material in which the group participates as a whole. It is a rewarding experience to move through this process with people who are empathetic to your needs.

Another helpful tip is to do some writing exercises as to what your feelings are revealing to you. You may elaborate on it with an art project and discuss it with a trained professional counselor to clarify how your writing and art console you. When feelings paralyze you, write down small goals you will fully commit to despite your despair. Completing a small goal can instill the needed confidence to go on. Goals for self-care will help you focus on moving forward, such as getting a haircut, buying a new suit, applying for a new job, or spending quality time with the children at the park. In addition, different surroundings may have you become aware of the beauty outside of you.

Lastly, it is vital that you write down affirmations to confirm your feelings. Some comforting affirmations are:

"It is ok that I feel sad."

"My anger is a healthy emotion that will move me to necessary action."

"Happiness is a decision I make despite my circumstances."

"I'm glad I feel my anger." "It allows me to know what is not ok."

It is a wise decision to get a coach after your counseling is complete for continued support. You're worth it!

CHECK OUT EVERYTHING

Are the procedures the bureaucratic clerk referring to valid?

How do you know what to believe?

Is the person in a position of power telling you accurate information?

When your soon-to-be ex agrees verbally, how much weight does that carry?

Are the procedures in your case being followed correctly?

These are questions to begin the process of checking out what is accurate information.

PROCESSES and PROCEDURES

When navigating a bureaucracy, it is critical to understand the procedures. One way to understand is to review the procedure manual. In most circumstances, the manual can be viewed upon request. Whatever method the clerk is referring to, you may identify it in the manual.

Ask the supervisor to help locate the procedure in the manual to save time. When a supervisor or clerk indicates anything regarding your case, suggest that the clerk put the statement in writing and have the clerk sign their name on the account along with their business phone number and email. Follow up with questions and ask for time frames for the answer in writing.

GOVERNING CONDUCT

In court matters, a person in power may be a judge, a magistrate, a mediator, an attorney, and other supporting staff. Research and understand the role and/or any code of conduct with which their behavior is governed. For example, If a judge seems to ignore your request to speak about the facts of your case, check out the judge's judicial code of conduct. Respectfully request to be heard according to the code of conduct. When a mediator pushes off the discussion of an earned income child tax credit in the current mediation, question: "Why postpone a discussion when we have the opportunity to agree in this mediation?"

Many times it is pure manipulation.

VERBAL PROMISES

Parents banter about what they promise to do during family issues with child support, divorce, and timesharing with children. One parent may take it seriously, and the other may not, especially when there is a court date to address the issues. However, you can ensure whatever promise was made is in writing and signed by both parties. It is easier when things are in writing.

HIGH STANDARDS

Lastly, ensure procedures in your case are followed, especially if you have a final judgment. If the other parent fails to abide by what was ordered, you may want to return to court. Act expeditiously to show it is important to you. Communicate and keep the standards high so everyone you interact with understands that you want success for your child, and you will follow through to achieve it perseveringly.

DOCUMENT EVERYTHING

A concerned parent is an aware parent. One way to ease your mind is to document incidences that you may need to recollect or use as evidence later. You may also use documentation to highlight your exemplary parenting skills. There are different forms of documentation to utilize. Remember to document the time and day and the nature of what happened. This documentation correlates with your binder; however, this is more specific and is similar to a diary. Here are some ideas to help you stay organized.

DOCUMENTING CONCERNS ABOUT THE OTHER PARENT'S QUESTIONABLE BEHAVIOR

* Anything that would threaten your child.

* Vulgar language used around your child.

* Disparaging comments about you to the child.

* Facebook videos and pictures depicting improper behavior for a parent.

* Welfare checks and follow-up appointments.

* Police reports.

* Child counseling reports.

* Safety hazards.

* Questionable people around the child.

* Comments from your child that may cause concern. "There is no food in the house."

* Bruises on your child.

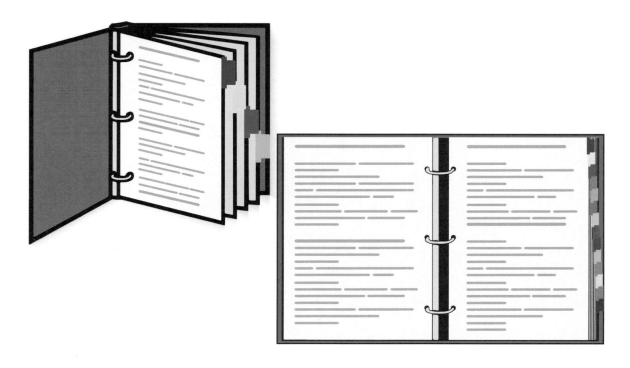

DOCUMENTING YOUR EXEMPLARY PARENTING SKILLS

* Outings at the park, beach, or zoo with your child.

* Pictures at a piano recital.

* Highlights of school events.

* A day shopping with your child.

* A letter from the daycare supervisor complimenting your parenting skills.

* Spending a couple of hours at a painting studio for quality time.

* A fun lunch out.

* Your volunteer work at your child's school.

* Quality reading/homework time to ensure good grades.

These forms of documentation will create more confidence in you because at any time you will have this information at your fingertips should you need to go back to court and prove what is necessary for the child's best interest.

DETAILED CATEGORY TIPS FOR YOUR BINDER TABS

1. CHILD'S SCHOOL INFO

Best to keep communication with your child's teacher current -at least twice per month (in writing), usually via email. Find out particulars on assignments, child's behavior, etc. Usually, children need to read for 20 minutes per night. Know the teacher's name, and if there is a major concern or incident with the child, email the teacher and copy the email to the school principal.

2. CHILD'S MEDICAL INFO

Keep current on your child's physicals, dental, vision, and any other concerns you hear from the child. Know the physician's name and the address of his office.

3. CHILD'S COUNSELOR REPORTS

This is important because, during a divorce or breakup, a child may experience grief. The child's feelings need to be validated by people who are equipped to do so. So often, parents are too emotional to acknowledge a child's grief. It is a true gift for a child to be able to speak with a neutral party who is trained in this field of psychology/counseling.

It is also important for a child to be able to speak with a counselor in regard to any abuse going on in the other parent's home. For example, domestic violence, subtle inappropriate behavior, and such. A child needs to know what normal is, and a counselor can help to shed light on the situation. Remember to get frequent reports. And have the reports explained to you.

4. CHILD'S SPECIAL NEEDS

Any special needs your child has, be it medical, psychological, nutritional, and/or educational, you may input behind this indicated tab.

5. WELFARE CHECKS ON CHILD

If you are concerned in regard to the child's safety, your community should have an 800 number to call for law enforcement to check on the child. You likely will need the child's address and be able to indicate what your concerns are.

One way to be thorough in communication with the staff is to ask for the case worker's name/email and the supervisor's name/email and copy both of them in the email with regard to time frames for obtaining a report.

6. COMMUNICATION WITH CHILD'S TEACHERS

Your child may have many different teachers. There are teachers for art, piano, sports, reading, singing, drama, and more. Stay in frequent touch in writing or document the lessons to show your commitment to your child's well-being. Periodically display your child's work to show how proud you are.

7. ONLINE COMMUNICATION BETWEEN YOU AND OTHER PARENT

There are venues of communication, such as www.talkingparents.com, that many of our customers use and can be incorporated into the parenting plan so that all the communication can be documented in writing. For any important or concerning communication, simply print it out and save it in your binder.

A way to communicate to avoid unnecessary slang no matter how you feel is to indicate: "Message received." I'll get back to you within _____." (state time frame) Or indicate: "Message received." "Will do." If the other parent is being inappropriate, remember this simplified response. You will look better if you behave in control of your emotions. And you will set a strong example for success. It may help the other parent learn what it is like to behave as a win/win!

8. TEXTING COMMUNICATION

If you feel comfortable and agree to text the other party, of course, be sure to be professional and print out any tests that are of concern.

9. POLICE REPORTS

Report any violent behavior and any no-shows for child timesharing. Report other incidences that create an issue for child safety. You may be able to use the evidence in court, and you may want to file a Petition for a change in the existing order to keep the child safe.

10. COURT MEDIATED AGREEMENT

It is important to review and highlight pertinent information in your mediated agreement, so you understand the time frames of timesharing with the child, communication requirements, out-of-state travel, and extra expenses for the child that you and the other parent will contribute to appropriately.

11. COURT ORDERED PARENTING PLAN AND FINAL JUDGMENT

Please read it thoroughly and ensure that each of you abides by the court order. If there are any unanticipated issues and you want to change the plan. For example, one parent has a substance abuse problem and is unsafe. You may want to go back to the court and request a change to the order.

12. STATUTES

It may be helpful to familiarize yourself with procedures/laws of the state (in regard to time-sharing with the child) just to become more informed and feel secure about what is allowed.

13. BACKGROUND CHECKS

Many times customers tell me that they are not certain who the other parent is living with as a mate. The person may have a felony record or a drug addiction and not be safe to be around children. You may do background checks to protect your child from an unsafe person. You may want to ask for a parenting plan in which the other parent has supervised time. It is common for parents in mediation to ask for supervised time with the child for a parent who has a mate with substance abuse problems.

14. DRUG AND ALCOHOL TESTING

Stay with any court-ordered drug and alcohol testing for both you and the other parent, and if applicable, print the results and add them to the binder. There are programs you may research to get additional help.

15. YOUR SUCCESSFUL TIME SHARING WITH CHILD

Document times, dates, and outings where you and your child have had fun times. You may also want to document piano class, art class, or any other activities that make great memories. If ever needed, it would be beneficial documentation to show you are an involved parent.

16. CHARACTER REFERENCES FOR YOU

Great references about YOU are nice to have on hand if the other parent is character-assassinating you. Show your great reputation by providing references about your character. Please have your professional friends check their spelling and have their signature notarized when writing their recommendations.

17. CHILD NUTRITION PLAN

If a child has a special nutrition plan, for example, no sugar due to Diabetes, the handout of the no food list should be in your binder. Be sure to educate anyone else who cares for the child as well. Post in the kitchen for the babysitter to see.

18. FEELINGS YOU HAVE ASSOCIATED WITH THIS PROCESS

This process of divorce or family court matters can be uncomfortable. It may benefit you to document your feelings as you move through the process. This would be a step to validate yourself, be it grief, anger, sadness, and the like.

19. COUNSELING TO BE THE BEST YOU CAN BE

If you need additional support, there are counselors to help assist with paving the way to a new start.

20. FUTURE GOALS

It is fun to think about how you would like your life to be after a divorce or breakup. Let the creativity flow so you can actualize your potential!

EXPECT RESISTANCE

Plan on facing resistance when seeking help with the case. It may seem befuddling as to why you would face resistance but there are a multitude of reasons to why people hesitate to assist you properly. When you choose to understand you depersonalize their behavior, thus persevering despite the circumstances.

Here are some reasons that were uncovered over the 23 years that I have studied employees behavior in child support offices, similar bureaucracies as well as court offices.

1. The agencies ability to function does not need a customer's direct monetary contribution as private sector business does.

2. People who are meant to assist you may naturally hesitate in order to weigh out the question in order to give a correct answer.

3. Some have the idea that to give you all the knowledge somehow depletes what knowledge is possessed by them. Maybe a win/loose or a loose/loose attitude.

4. A person may choose the governmental job to be able to "end" the workday at a certain time. The job is not a passionate choice. The goal for excellent customer service was not the reason the job was chosen.

5. In order to perform with excellence one needs to manage oneself with consistent energy. Frankly the people who resist your needs may not have what it takes.

6. In a court and child support system the general atmosphere is that of "something went wrong." For instance: Someone failed to pay child support. A husband and wife failed at a marriage. Parents failed to care properly for their child. Employees may negatively judge you and think you deserve to be treated in a derogatory way. There may be a shame associated with failure.

7. The employee may neglect his own goals and desires. If that is true, why would he want to assist you properly when he does not even assist himself?

8. Improper training of staff. Sometimes excellent service is as easy as learning a skill with a smile and eye contact. If management does not emphasize exemplary training then you surely will get resistance.

Knowing these reasons for resistance in relation to your family court matter will reduce the stress by seeing the employee with empathy. It may also eliminate the shock value and allow you to prepare ahead of time and assure your goals get accomplished for your case.

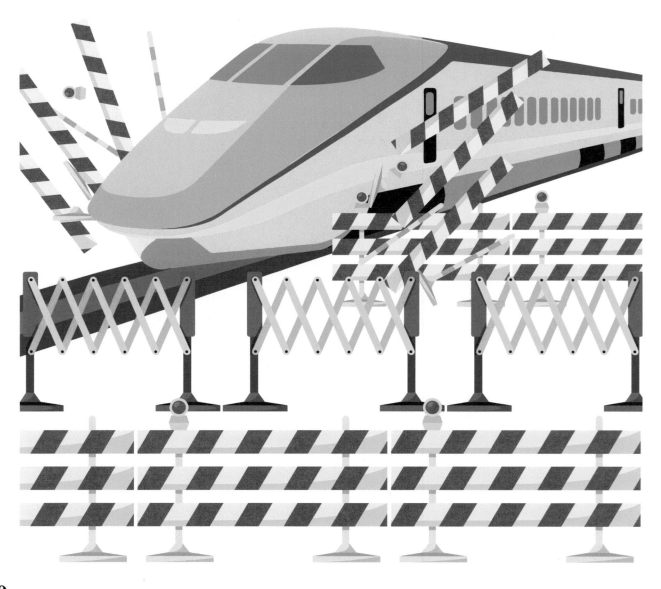

Printed in the United States
by Baker & Taylor Publisher Services